DINO RIZZO

REACH
PEOPLE
MOVEMENT

SMALL GROUP CURRICULUM

ISBN: 978-1-64296-027-3

Published by Servolution

Printed in the United States

TABLE OF
CONTENTS

INTRODUCTION

Welcome to RPM — Reach People Movement! We are so excited you're coming to the table for this discussion. This study was created to stir up your passion for serving others and to equip you with confidence and practical tools to reach the people around you with the love of Jesus in a way that impacts their lives for eternity.

Our foundational Scripture for RPM is **Acts 10:38 NIV**:

> "...how God anointed Jesus of Nazareth **with the Holy Spirit** and power, and how **He went around doing good** and **healing** all who were under the power of the devil, because **God was with Him.**"

Jesus is the perfect example of someone who lived a powerful life of outreach. He was full of the power of the Holy Spirit, and His life was marked by the good things He did for others. And of course, everywhere He went, with every good work, He spread the message of the Gospel. As

He served people — healing the sick, feeding the hungry, and bringing freedom to the oppressed--He continually preached the truth that God loved them, God valued them, and the Son of God (He) had come to save them. We are called to live this way and proclaim this same Good News to everyone we encounter, because every person matters to God!

Throughout this 6-week study, we will talk about how to reach people in effective, practical ways. Every small group meeting will include a video session hosted by Dino Rizzo, who is a pastor, a ministry leader, and the founder of an international outreach effort called "Servolution." Dino will share a brief thought and passage of Scripture at the beginning of each session and then interview various ministry leaders who are passionate about outreach in many different forms. After the video portion of your small group meeting, you will have the opportunity to talk about that week's interview together and go through a series of Discussion Questions. At the end of your meeting, your leader will review the weekly Action Step and challenge you to put your takeaways from the session into action during the week. Be sure to lean into these Action Steps over the next 6 weeks so that you can grow in your ability to reach people. That's what this is all about!

There is a list of "25 Practical Ideas for Reaching People" on Page 45 of this book. Consider picking a few of these ideas to do as a group over the course of this study. Of course, you can do as many of them as you want on your own, but try to find ways to serve people together as well. You'll be amazed by what you can accomplish when you work as a team.

Ready to dive in, learn, grow, and reach people with the love of Jesus? Let's get started!

Access each week's video at servolution.org/rpm.

REACHING PEOPLE WITH EVANGELISM

WELCOME · — — · — — · — — · — — · — — · — — ·

It's Week 1 of *RPM — Reach People Movement* — and today, we're focusing on the ultimate purpose behind all of our outreach efforts: telling people about the Good News of Jesus Christ. As Christians, we are called to share the love of Jesus with others in a way that impacts them for eternity. This act of sharing our faith is called "evangelism."

Don't be intimidated by the word "evangelism." It isn't as complicated as it might seem. Evangelism isn't something that only vocational ministers are qualified to do. Evangelism is for everyone. We don't have to make grand gestures or communicate perfectly or know everything about the Bible to effectively reach people with the Gospel. That isn't what Jesus asks of us. He simply asks us to connect with the people we encounter in our everyday lives and share His love with them. No matter where we are, there is always someone who needs Jesus. We just need to have eyes to see them and the confidence to reach out to them.

SCRIPTURE · — — · — — · — — · — — · — — ·

So [Jesus] came to a town in Samaria called Sychar, near the plot of ground Jacob had given to his son Joseph. Jacob's well was there, and Jesus, tired as He was from the journey, sat down by the well. It was about noon. When a Samaritan woman came to draw water, Jesus said to her, "Will you give me a drink?"...

The Samaritan woman said to Him, "You are a Jew and I am a Samaritan woman. How can You ask me for a drink?" (For Jews do not associate with Samaritans.)

Jesus answered her, "If you knew the gift of God and who it is that asks you for a drink, you would have asked Him and He would have given you living water." "Sir," the woman said, "You have nothing to draw with and the well is deep. Where can You get this living water? Are You greater than our father Jacob, who gave us the well and drank from it himself, as did also his sons and his livestock?"

Jesus answered, "Everyone who drinks this water will be thirsty again, but whoever drinks the water I give them will never thirst. Indeed, the water I give them will become in them a spring of water welling up to eternal life."

The woman said to Him, "Sir, give me this water so that I won't get thirsty and have to keep coming here to draw water."

He told her, "Go, call your husband and come back."

"I have no husband," she replied.

Jesus said to her, "You are right when you say you have no husband. The fact is, you have had five husbands, and the man you now have is not your husband. What you have just said is quite true."

"Sir," the woman said, "I can see that You are a prophet...

The woman said, "I know that Messiah" (called Christ) "is coming. When He comes, He will explain everything to us."

Then Jesus declared, "I, the one speaking to you—I am He."...

Then, leaving her water jar, the woman went back to the town and said to the people, "Come, see a man who told me everything I ever did. Could this be the Messiah?"

— FROM JOHN 4 NIV

SESSION ONE NOTES ·━ ·━━ ━ · ━ ━ · ━ ━ · ·

In this week's interview, Dino Rizzo interviews J. John, a speaker, writer, and evangelist from Chorleywood, England, who lives out this life of daily evangelism in powerful, practical ways. Take notes on their discussion below.

....

....

....

....

....

....

....

....

....

....

....

....

....

....

....

....

....

....

....

SESSION ONE NOTES · ▬ ▪▪▬ ▬ ▪ ▬ ▪ ▬ ▪ ▪

....

....

....

....

....

....

....

....

....

....

....

....

....

....

....

....

....

....

....

....

....

DISCUSSION QUESTIONS ·—·—— — · — — · ··

- What was one of your biggest takeaways from Dino's interview with J. John?

- J. John mentioned that Jesus used what He had in common with the Samaritan woman — water — to connect in conversation with her and then connect her to the truth of the Gospel. How can finding something in common with another person be helpful in your efforts to reach them with the Gospel?

- Let's talk about J. John's process of reaching out to the billionaire. What stuck out to you about his story? How can you develop the patience and perseverance to continue to reach out to those who reject the Gospel when you present it? How can you practically pursue those who are resistant to the Gospel?

- J. John said, "Christianity is essentially about three things: forgiveness from the past, new life here today, and a hope for the future." Which of these three things is easiest for you to communicate to others? Which is the most challenging?

ACTION STEP · — — · — — · — — · — — · — — ·

Go through this week with your eyes open to the people around you. Ask the Holy Spirit to lead you to people with whom He wants you to share the message of God's love and forgiveness. Be purposeful in your connection with them, and confidently share the truth of the Gospel with them.

PRAYER ·— —·— —·— —·— —·— —·

God, thank You for letting us partner with You in expanding Your Kingdom. We pray for fresh opportunities to share Your love with the people around us. Remind us every day of the joy of the Good News, and give us confidence to share it with the people we encounter. Lead us in our conversations with others so we can build strong connections and effectively communicate the Gospel. In Jesus' Name, Amen.

IF WE WANT TO **SHARE THE GOSPEL** **WITH CONFIDENCE,** WE HAVE TO **HAVE CONFIDENCE,** *IN THE* GOSPEL.

J. JOHN

SESSION TWO

REACHING THE ONE

During this second session of RPM, we're focusing on reaching the one. It's incredible to think that the God who created the universe cares deeply about every individual person on earth. He sees each of our personal needs and desires for them to be met. And He designed the Church to be His hands and feet to meet those needs and to care for the poor, the hurting, and the oppressed. This is our calling: to seek out the one, help them however we can, and bring them to Jesus.

Understanding God's love for the one will motivate us to intentionally find ways to reach them. God doesn't want a single one of us to be outside of a relationship with Him, and He sent His Son to make a way for every person to draw near to Him and know Him. Serving others gives us a unique opportunity to share this truth in a way that changes lives forever. When we see and meet someone's individual needs, we will find that they are more open to receiving the Gospel. Demonstrating the love of God on a personal level is one of the most powerful ways we can reach the lost.

SCRIPTURE · — — · — — · — — · — — · — — ·

"If a man owns a hundred sheep, and one of them wanders away, will he not leave the ninety-nine on the hills and go to look for the one that wandered off? And if he finds it, truly I tell you, he is happier about that one sheep than about the ninety-nine that did not wander off. In the same way your Father in heaven is not willing that any of these little ones should perish."
— MATTHEW 18:12-14 NIV

SESSION TWO 15

The Lord is not slow in keeping His promise, as some understand slowness. Instead He is patient with you, not wanting anyone to perish, but everyone to come to repentance.

— 2 PETER 3:9 NIV

SESSION TWO NOTES · ━ ━ ━ ━ · ━ ━ · ━ ━ · ·

In this week's interview, Dino Rizzo interviews Tori Townley, a visionary leader with the outreach effort "Servolution," who lives every day in search of the one. Take notes on their discussion below.

....

....

....

....

....

....

....

....

....

....

....

....

....

....

....

SESSION TWO NOTES · — — -- — · — · — · ·

DISCUSSION QUESTIONS ·—--— — · — — · ··

o What was one of your biggest takeaways from Dino's interview with Tori?

o Tori talked about the importance of recognizing our own dignity so that we can ascribe dignity to others. What barriers might keep you from fully receiving the dignity and identity you have in Christ? Does the way you currently see yourself affect the way you treat others?

o What does it look like to be led by the Holy Spirit as we go throughout our day?

o Do you tend to naturally notice individual needs around you, or do you need to be intentional to look for the one? What can you do weekly to serve the one?

ACTION STEP · — — · — — · — — · — — · — — ·

Look at the list of 25 Practical Ways to Serve People in the back of this book. Choose one idea, and make plans to serve someone in that way this week. As you serve, be intentional about looking for one individual person with whom you can share the love of Jesus.

PRAYER · — — · — — · — — · — — · — — ·

God, thank You for wanting every single one of us to know You. Give us Your heart for the one so that we can go through each day aware of the people around us who need to know You. Help us to see ourselves the way You see us, so we can then ascribe proper worth and dignity to others. Show us who You want us to serve this week, and give us courage to reach out to them. In Jesus' Name, Amen.

REACH THE WORLD BY *SERVING* ONE.

TORI TOWNLEY

REACHING PEOPLE BY BUILDING A BRIDGE

In this week's session of RPM, we're focusing on building bridges. A bridge connects two places that were once separated, and that is the essence of Jesus in the Gospel. He knew that people needed to be reconnected to God, so He continuously got close to others, met them where they were, and created connections to bring people to a full life in relationship with God. Now, He asks us to do the same. He's given us the privilege of connecting with others — building a bridge — so that they can connect back to Him.

It may be difficult for us to imagine getting close with certain people in a society that is so polarized by its differences. In an age of heightened hostility, we have to approach building a bridge with a spirit of humility. With a humble posture, we can effectively enter into other people's worlds, listen to them, learn from them, and find common ground. As we meet people where they are and cultivate connection through our availability, service, empathy, and genuine desire for relationship, we will be able to walk alongside them on a pathway that leads to Jesus.

SCRIPTURE ·— —·— —·— —·— —·— —·

...I have become a slave to all people to bring many to Christ. When I was with the Jews, I lived like a Jew to bring the Jews to Christ. When I was with those who follow the Jewish law, I too lived under that law. Even though I am not subject to the law, I did this so I could bring to Christ those who are under the law. When I am with the Gentiles who do not follow the Jewish law, I too live apart from that law so I can bring them to Christ. But I do not ignore the law of God; I obey the law

of Christ. When I am with those who are weak, I share their weakness, for I want to bring the weak to Christ. Yes, I try to find common ground with everyone, doing everything I can to save some.
— I CORINTHIANS 9:19-22 NLT

SESSION THREE NOTES· ————··—— ·— —— ·— —— ··

In this week's interview, Dino Rizzo interviews Edwin Jones, the lead pastor of The Bridge Church in Hampton, Virginia, whose heart and mission are to connect people to God through relationships. Take notes on their discussion below.

....

....

....

....

....

....

....

....

....

....

....

....

....

....

....

SESSION THREE NOTES ·—·—··—··—·—··—··

DISCUSSION QUESTIONS · —·— — · — — · ··

o What was one of your biggest takeaways from this interview?

o Edwin said that the only thing that can combat a spirit of hostility is a spirit of humility. What does it look like to approach someone who thinks, looks, or acts differently than you with a spirit of humility? How can you cultivate humility in your daily interactions with people?

o Have you experienced a time when loving or reaching someone felt uncomfortable because of your differences? When this happens, how can you shift your focus to the joy of meeting their physical and spiritual needs?

o Edwin said God has given each of us unique abilities to reach people in our own way. Does knowing there's no "right" way to do it help you feel more comfortable and confident about outreach? How do you think God has uniquely wired you to reach people?

ACTION STEP · — — · — — · — — · — — · — — ·

As you interact with others this week, be intentional about building strong connections. Take on a spirit of humility, and meet people right where they are. Ask the Holy Spirit to lead you as you develop these relationships so that you can know the best way to build a bridge for each person to connect with Jesus.

PRAYER · — — · — — · — — · — — · — — ·

God, thank You for designing us with the ability to reach people in a unique way and for giving us the privilege of connecting others to You. Help us to meet people right where they are today. Give us a spirit of humility so we can care for others well and find common ground. Help us to build bridges that allow others to connect with You in a way that changes their lives forever, for Your glory. In Jesus' Name, Amen.

CONNECT WITH **PEOPLE** SO YOU CAN **CONNECT THEM** TO CHRIST.

EDWIN JONES

REACHING PEOPLE WITH AUTHENTICITY

In today's session, we're talking about reaching people with authenticity. There is a common pressure many of us feel as Christians: a need to "have it all together" in order to be qualified to serve others. The truth is, our greatest ability to reach people often comes from our willingness to serve in and through our weaknesses. When God called us to love our neighbors, He already knew all the ways we would fail and struggle in different areas of our lives. When we share those struggles and experiences with others, they have the opportunity to see the power of God's grace and mercy at work in our lives. Knowing that we are imperfect and only made righteous by Jesus will help our fellow imperfect friends and neighbors see that His grace and mercy are available to them, too.

When we are open about our personal need for Christ, the people around us will feel safe and understood. As we connect over our shared imperfections and our shared need for Jesus, we will lay a foundation for genuine friendships that can then lead to our friends developing a genuine relationship with God.

SCRIPTURE ·━━·━━·━━·━━·━━·

I thank Christ Jesus our Lord, who has given me strength to do His work. He considered me trustworthy and appointed me to serve Him, even though I used to blaspheme the name of Christ. In my insolence, I persecuted His people. But God had mercy on me because I did it in ignorance and unbelief. Oh, how generous and gracious our Lord was! He filled me with the faith and love that come from Christ Jesus.

This is a trustworthy saying, and everyone should accept it: "Christ Jesus came into the world to save sinners"—and I am the worst of them all. But God had mercy on me so that Christ Jesus could use me as a prime example of His great patience with even the worst sinners. Then others will realize that they, too, can believe in Him and receive eternal life. **— I TIMOTHY 1:12-16 NLT**

SESSION FOUR NOTES ·━━━-━ ·━ ━ ·━ ━ · ·

In this week's interview, Dino Rizzo interviews Holly Wagner, a pastor, author, and speaker who has spent her life spreading the Gospel by sharing her authentic self with others. Take notes on their discussion below.

....

....

....

....

....

....

....

....

....

....

....

....

....

....

....

....

SESSION FOUR NOTES ·———··——·—··

DISCUSSION QUESTIONS ·———·—— — · — — · ··

- What was one of your biggest takeaways from this interview?

- Thinking back over the last year of your life, what is something God has done in you or helped you walk through that you can share with the people around you? How do you think sharing that experience will help others see Jesus?

- Holly said that God trusts us with the broken, so we need to be patient with them. Do you tend to rush people to change? What can you do to slow down, relate to people where they are, and embrace the pace of the journey on which God is taking them?

- Your background, gifts, personality, and life experience all work together to give you unique, dynamic ways to serve and relate to others. How do you think these factors in your life have specifically equipped you to reach people?

ACTION STEP · ·— — · — — · — — · — — · — — ·

Take time this week to practice sharing your testimony and the ways God has moved or is moving in your life in just a few sentences. Not every interaction we have is going to give us a lot of time, but we can still make a big impact if we learn to share our stories well.

PRAYER · — — · — — · — — · — — · — — ·

God, thank You for giving us grace so that we can share it with others. Give us boldness to be authentic, to share our struggles, and to experience real life with the people You place in our paths. Help us show others the power of Your grace and mercy in our lives so that they can experience that power in their lives, too. In Jesus' Name, Amen.

 WE DON'T
HAVE TO HAVE
ALL OUR STUFF
TOGETHER;
WE JUST
HAVE TO BE
HONEST.

HOLLY WAGNER

REACHING THE NEXT GENERATION

Today's session is all about reaching the next generation and involving young people in our outreach efforts. What the next generation needs from us more than anything is an authentic belief in them. They need someone to acknowledge and care about their individual needs, and they need people to see and believe in their potential. As we reach out to young people, we should always look for opportunities to speak to their potential and encourage them that God has a plan for their lives. It's so important for the next generation to know God! They are the future of the Church and the future of the world — and God wants every young person to experience His love and receive salvation.

In addition to reaching the next generation, we need to encourage young believers to join us as we serve and reach out to others. No one is too young to be used by God. Let's encourage the young people around us to be actively involved in outreach! As we teach them to reach others and serve their community, they will not only make a difference today but become equipped to lead the future Church in sharing the love of Jesus in powerful, practical ways.

SCRIPTURE · — — · — — · — — · — — · — — ·

Don't let anyone look down on you because you are young, but set an example for the believers in speech, in conduct, in love, in faith and in purity.   **— I TIMOTHY 1:12-16 NIV**

SESSION FIVE NOTES · — - -- — · - — · - — · ·

In this week's interview, Dino Rizzo interviews Chris Durso, a pastor, author, and speaker whose approach to reaching the next generation has impacted the Church around the world. Take notes on their discussion.

....

....

....

....

....

....

....

....

....

....

....

....

....

....

....

....

....

....

....

....

SESSION FIVE NOTES ·━ ·━ ·· ━ ·━ ━ ·━ ··

....
....
....
....
....
....
....
....
....
....
....
....
....
....
....
....
....
....
....
....
....
....
....
....

DISCUSSION QUESTIONS ·—·—·—·—·—·—··

- What was one of your biggest takeaways from Dino's interview with Chris?

- Chris talked about the importance of empathy and relating to what young people experience in order to reach them effectively. Do you tend to dismiss the feelings of young people? How can you more actively listen to the next generation and show that you care about their current perspectives and emotions?

- We need to be intentional about getting the next generation involved in outreach. What kinds of serve projects are great opportunities for children and teenagers to participate? How can you help the young people around you develop a heart for outreach from a young age?

- Brainstorm some ideas for reaching the next generation in your community. How can you connect with and serve young people in practical ways?

ACTION STEP ·—·—·—·—·—·—·—·—·

Take time this week to pour into a young person in your family or community. Speak to their potential, and encourage them with the truth that God has a plan for their life. If you are a young person, invite a friend to participate in a serve project with you. You can make a difference and help others do the same!

PRAYER ·—·—·—·—·—·—·—·

God, thank You for giving us grace so that we can share it with others. Give us boldness to be authentic, to share our struggles, and to experience real life with the people You place in our paths. Help us show others the power of Your grace and mercy in our lives so that they can experience that power in their lives, too. In Jesus' Name, Amen.

THE MOMENT
YOU **RECOGNIZE**
A TEENAGER AS
AN INDIVIDUAL
WITH
REAL
NEEDS,
THEY WILL
ENGAGE
IN THE
CONVERSATION
WITH YOU.

CHRIS DURSO

REACHING PEOPLE WITH INTENTIONALITY

In this final session of RPM, we're focusing on reaching people with intentionality. One of the greatest keys to living an impactful life that reaches others is good stewardship of our time. We need to use the moments God has given us to share the love of Jesus with as many people as possible. Jesus spent His life "doing good" for people: spending His time and attention focusing on the needs of others, helping people in both practical and spiritual ways. Because we are filled with the Holy Spirit, we are equipped to follow His example.

We can serve people best by being aware of not only their physical needs but their emotional needs as well. Part of stewarding our time well is creating margin to be present with people in their pain. By listening and carrying the peaceful, powerful presence of God with us, we can help people heal. When we are intentional to focus on the people, and not just the serve project, we can demonstrate the heart of Jesus in a way that will change their lives forever.

SCRIPTURE · — — · — — · — — · — — · — — ·

"...how God anointed Jesus of Nazareth with the Holy Spirit and power, and how He went around doing good and healing all who were under the power of the devil, because God was with Him."

— ACTS 10:38

SESSION SIX NOTES ·— —-- — ·- — ·- — ···

In this week's interview, Dino Rizzo interviews Tim Timberlake, a pastor, speaker, and author who intentionally stewards the minutes he's given each day to reach as many people as possible. Take notes on their discussion below.

....

....

....

....

....

....

....

....

....

....

....

....

....

....

....

....

....

....

....

SESSION SIX NOTES

....
....
....
....
....
....
....
....
....
....
....
....
....
....
....
....
....
....
....
....
....
....

DISCUSSION QUESTIONS ·————— — · — — · ··

o What was one of your biggest takeaways from this interview?

o Do you think you are currently a good steward of your time? What are some practical ways you can be more intentional with your time in order to reach others?

o Sometimes, because we're focused on meeting someone's practical needs, we can forget to focus on the person we're trying to help and ultimately reach. As you participate in outreach projects, what can you do to make sure the person you're serving personally experiences the love of Jesus?

o Tim said we carry the person of Jesus through the power of our presence. How can the simple act of listening impact others? How does this kind of personal attention and care reflect the heart of God?

ACTION STEP · - — · - — · - — · - — · - —·

As a group, identify an opportunity to serve your community together this week. Learn about the practical needs of people in your community, taking into consideration local schools, unhoused individuals, and the people in your own neighborhoods and congregations. Make a plan, make it happen, and be intentional to steward your time and attention to connect with people as you serve them. Remember: It's all about **people**!

PRAYER · — — · — — · — — · — — · — —·

God, thank You for giving us 1,440 minutes every day. Give us wisdom to steward them well. Help us be aware of the needs of our community, and help us find solutions. As we meet those needs, give us opportunities to share Your love with others. Help us focus on people first and then the task at hand. Make us effective in reaching people, for Your glory. In Jesus' Name, Amen.

FIND THE
PROBLEM,
PROVIDE A
SOLUTION,
AND THEN INFUSE
TRANSFORMATION
THROUGH THE
GOSPEL
OF
JESUS
CHRIST.

TIM TIMBERLAKE

25

PRACTICAL IDEAS

for

REACHING PEOPLE

1. Deliver pizza to single parents and their families.

2. Leave bags of treats and handwritten notes for your delivery drivers.

3. Deliver essentials kits to local shelters for people experiencing homelessness.

4. Voice-record personal prayers for friends and family and send them via text.

5. Deliver care packages to medical care heroes at local hospitals.

6. Offer to take free family portraits for people in your community.

7. Drop off free breakfast and treats to drivers at truck stops.

8. Set up a stand at a laundromat to give out quarters, detergent, dryer sheets, and snacks.

9. Start a pen-pal program with local assisted living residents.

10. Offer to pay for someone's gas at the pump.

11. Surprise shoppers at your local grocery story by paying for their groceries.

12. Fill the employee break rooms at local businesses with snacks, flowers, and "thank you" signs.

13. Drive thru your favorite fast food restaurant, but skip the order! Instead — GIVE the employees at the window a sweet surprise they'll never forget.

14. Check out a Redbox Movie, insert a few dollars and a note back in the case, and return it to bless the next person.

15. Bring goodies to local first responders.

16. Put together a dinner kit for a family going through a busy or difficult season.

17. Donate blood to your local blood bank.

18. Bring gift bags to families with babies in the NICU.

19. Host a fun activity night for children who have special needs and simultaneously bless their parents with free babysitting and an evening out!

20. Host a free car wash.

21. Do a room makeover for someone who could use an uplifting refresh.

22. Bring energy drinks to construction workers or linemen.

23. Throw a surprise birthday party for someone - even though it's not their birthday.

24. Take time to really listen to someone's story. Let them know they're heard, cherished, and loved.

25. Use your talent! If you like to write, send a poem to a friend. If you like to go fishing, share your catches with a neighbor. If you like to draw, create pieces of art and notes of encouragement to send to individuals who are incarcerated.

ADDITIONAL RESOURCES .__.._ _ . _ _ . ..

Follow **@servolution** on Instagram for serve ideas and inspiration.

For local serve opportunities near you, download **The Serve App.** Available on all mobile platforms.

THANK YOU

FROM DINO RIZZO

Thank you to my wife, DeLynn, and my amazing children.

Thank you to everyone who contributed to this curriculum and live out this Reach People Movement every day - J. John, Tori Townley, Edwin Jones, Holly Wagner, Chris Durso, Tim Timberlake, Julio Melara, Benny and Wendy Perez.

Thank you to these churches and organizations that model and support Servolution - Hand of Hope, Milestone Church, Fellowship Church, Lifepoint Church, Victory Family Church, River Valley Church, Hope City Church, Rez Church, Church of the Redeemer, Peoples Church, One Hope, Kingdom Builders, Church of the Highlands.

Thank you to all of those who work on our Serve Team, the ARC Team, my pastor Chris Hodges, and the wonderful people of Church of the Highlands.

MORE FROM OUR GUESTS

J. JOHN
- 📷 🐦 @canonjjohn
- 🖥 www.canonjjohn.com

TORI TOWNLEY
- 🖥 www.serveday.com

EDWIN JONES
- 📷 @_edwinjones
- 🖥 www.thebridgechurchva.com

HOLLY WAGNER
- 📷 @hollywagnerla

CHRIS DURSO
- 📷 @chrisdurso
- 🖥 www.saintschurch.com

TIM TIMBERLAKE
- 📷 @ttimberlake
- 🖥 www.celebrationjax.org

JULIO MELARA
- 📷 @juliomelara

BENNY & WENDY PEREZ
- 📷 @bennyperez
- 📷 @wendyperez

SERVOLUTION
RESOURCES

GET YOUR COPY TODAY
ARCCHURCHES.COM

SERVE DAY

Serve Day is a yearly, worldwide outreach day that encourages churches and organizations all over the world to serve their local communities and share the love of God through practical acts of kindness. With practical tips and guided outreach ideas from the Servolution team, our hope is that serving grows beyond a single-day event. Our prayer is that Serve Day ignites a movement that reflects the kindness of Jesus and focuses on serving others every day. Simple acts of selfless love can open hearts to Jesus, and together we can make a difference.

To register your church, organization or yourself for Serve Day, and to learn more about our Serve Day resources, visit SERVEDAY.COM.

Association of Related Churches

To find resources on church planting, books, articles, stories, webinars, partner organizations, and more, visit

EQUIP.ARCCHURCHES.COM